Fellowship
of
Prayer

Lenten Season
1993

Sandy Dixon
and
Michael E. Dixon

Chalice Press
St. Louis, Missouri

Sandy Dixon is a staff member at Christian Board of Publication. A graduate of Culver Stockton College, she also attended Christian Theological Seminary. Sandy is the author of *We Rejoice in the Light*, and has contributed to *The Secret Place*, *The Disciple*, *Partners in Prayer*, and *Clergy Journal*.

Michael E. Dixon is an ordained minister in the Christian Church (Disciples of Christ) and a curriculum editor at Christian Board of Publication. He has written *Bread of Blessing, Cup of Hope* and youth curriculum courses in the areas of worship, symbols, religious drama, church history, and the Bible.

Mike and Sandy have three grown children and one grandson. They are active members at Northside Christian Church in St. Louis.

Introduction

Lent is a time of pilgrimage, a time for spiritual journeys. It is a time of discipline, a time of reflection, a time for deepening our faith. Our journey is with the Christ, the one who came that we might know abundant life and God's abundant love. Obviously, a major goal of our journey is to learn more about our traveling companion.

The Gospel According to John offers us a theological and spiritual portrait of the Christ. In this Gospel, claims are made about the Christ. These claims are often expressed when Jesus begins a sentence with "I am.... " These words remind readers of the God who appeared before Moses at the burning bush, who claimed the name "I AM WHO I AM." Jesus was not claiming to be God, but was demonstrating his closeness to God.

Using "I am..." as our road sign, our Lenten journey will begin with the God of the Hebrew Bible and then travel through John's Gospel. We will follow the statements in order, but when we arrive at each one we will explore some side roads and reflect upon some other scriptures that help us understand who our traveling companion is. The meditations for Holy Week, however, will look back upon various "I am" passages and not be in sequence.

The two of us have been on a Lenten journey of our own in writing these meditations. We have smiled at old memories, been startled by new insights, and wrestled with what it means to be part of a fellowship of prayer. May you be as blessed by the journey as we have been.

Sandy and Michael Dixon

Here I Am

Read Exodus 3:1–7.

God called to him out of the bush, "Moses, Moses!" And he said, "Here I am" (Exodus 3:4).

Moses needed to keep a low profile. He was a refugee, wanted for murder, and the desert became his refuge. The former prince of Egypt married into a shepherd's clan, and found in the vast quietness of the Sinai the peace that had eluded him in the palace.

Then one day, he saw a bush. It was ablaze, but still intact. He could have walked on by, ignoring it, pretending he didn't see. He could have run away, terrified. Instead, he approached it, wanting to understand. Approaching the bush, Moses encountered the presence of God. The scrub desert land was filled with this presence and transformed into a holy place. Moses was called by name, told to take off his sandals, for he was treading on holy ground, and warned not to come closer to the divine power. Moses answered the call. "Here I am." In the emptiness of a desert, he was ready to receive the word of God.

Ash Wednesday is a special time, just as the desert mountain slope was a special place. If we go to an Ash Wednesday service, or if we just set aside some time for prayer and reflection, this day can be a time when we can respond "Here I am" to the invitation of God. We may have been running away from a troubled past, like Moses. We may have been feeling trapped in a dry and barren place in our lives. In any case, this can be a day when our wandering becomes a journey of faith, a journey that begins when we are perceptive enough and brave enough to answer God's call to a new beginning, "Here I am."

Here I am, O God. Help me hear your call. Help me to be aware of your holiness and respond accordingly. Amen.

God Is—and That's Enough

Read Exodus 3:7–15.

God said to Moses, "I AM WHO I AM." He said further, "Thus you shall say to the Israelites, 'I AM has sent you'" (Exodus 3:14).

A common bush became a place where God was revealed. Moses listened in awe as this God of flame and light made connections with Moses' ancestors. This God had promised Abraham and Sarah a great people and a great land. This God was disturbed and distressed that this people was now a landless, oppressed colony of slaves. This God intended to go one-on-one with the Egyptian Pharaoh to rescue the slaves.

Yet slaves often have their cultural memories and identities stolen away by their owners. Would the Hebrews even remember this God of their far-removed ancestors, since they were now surrounded by powerful foreign deities? How could Moses get the people to listen? God's response was very simple, yet so very deep. "I AM WHO I AM. Tell them 'I AM' sent you."

God is—and that's enough. God doesn't need a name by which to be set apart from other gods. No one else can determine what or who God is—God is God. Behind all creation, behind everything, God is. This God had made a covenant, and the weight of the universe was behind it. That would be enough to lead the people to freedom.

Reflect for a moment. Name some of the gods of the culture around you, forces that threaten to enslave you. In the midst of these overwhelming "realities" there is the ultimate reality—the God who wants you to be truly free. The God who is.

Sometimes we forget you, O God. Help us be aware of the power of your name and the reality of your love. Amen.

Friday, February 26, 1993

God's Mighty Hand

Read Exodus 6:1–13.

"I will redeem you with an outstretched arm and with mighty acts of judgment. I will take you as my people, and I will be your God "(Exodus 6:6b–7a).

The Iron Curtain has fallen—was it economic and social forces, or is God at work? Dictators fall in bloodless coups—was it social unrest and internal dry rot, or is God at work? Acts of healing love bring peace to strife-torn families or congregations—was it just people at their best, or is God at work?

There are blind social and economic forces that shape and sometimes warp our lives and our cultures. There is human freedom that we can use to bring life and peace, or to bring destruction and judgment to our families or our congregations. As we read the story of Exodus, however, we find a faith statement. God isn't at some master control panel making everything happen according to a predestined plan. God is working through people—Moses, Aaron, slaves, and even through Pharaoh—in specific ways. God is, and God has a claim on us. God can use us, with all our gifts and our weaknesses, to bring freedom and hope. That God is still in our midst today.

God of freedom and hope, let me see your presence in the midst of our confused world. Amen.

Hello!

Read Psalm 91.

When they call to me, I will answer them (Psalm 91:15).

For over twelve years, I have worked on the telephone. Each day I go to work and call ministers to offer them information about new resources that may help them in their ministry. On many days I receive from the phone companies messages such as this: "I'm sorry, all circuits are busy"; "the area code has been changed..."; "the number has been disconnected"; "we can't complete your call as dialed. If you feel you have made an error, hang up and try again"; "If you feel you have reached this number in error, please contact your directory or call your operator."

It's not easy to reach my customers. Sometimes they are on another phone call, out of the office, in a conference, in staff meetings, or on their day off.

"I AM WHO I AM," says the Lord our God. This Psalm doesn't portray God as being as fickle as a phone system, offering varying messages that prevent one from completing the call. Instead, I AM WHO I AM, our refuge and fortress, our God in whom we trust, promises that when we call, we will be answered.

However great our technology in communication, it is fallible. I AM, God, is always there ready to answer, to listen, to protect, and to love.

Thank you, God, for the assurance of your protection, trustworthiness, availability, and salvation. Amen.

Our Journey

Read Isaiah 40:1–11.

A voice cries out: "In the wilderness prepare the way of the LORD" (Isaiah 40:3).

Guide me, O thou great Jehovah,
Pilgrim through this barren land;

Lent is a journey. We journey as the Hebrews did through a barren land. We journey from the light and celebration of Advent through the barrenness of an uncertain outcome.

I am weak, but thou are mighty,
Hold me with thy powerful hand;

We are uncertain of our direction; our way is rough. There is a wilderness in our lives that needs calming, taming. We are vague about how to do the penitent reflections of the season.

How can we acknowledge our dependence on God?

Bread of heaven, bread of heaven,
Feed me till I want no more;

We need to accept, in our wilderness journey, the bread from heaven as did the Hebrews. The literal meaning of *manna* is, "What is it?" The Israelites received nourishment and survived. We can accept God's manna also, in Jesus the bread of life. And in our journey, the difficult parts can be softened, the low parts of our journey leveled out, and the rough places made smooth.

Bread of heaven,
Feed me till I want no more.

Our bread of heaven is Jesus. Let us journey together.

As we pilgrim through this season toward new life, guide us in our struggles. Amen.

Monday, March 1, 1993

A Spring of Living Water

Read John 4:1–15.

"The water that I will give will become in them a spring of water gushing up to eternal life" (John 4:14).

The springs of southern Missouri refresh and renew our spirits. These beautiful blue pools of water are peaceful, yet ever active, as thousands of gallons of water flow upward every hour from the porous limestone beneath. The clear water is cold, providing a habitat for trout and watercress. As we walk along their banks, we feel that we are experiencing a parable of God's grace surging up into our lives.

Missouri has a wet climate, Israel a dry one. We drive to the springs in air-conditioned autos; they walked dry dusty trails. It is no wonder that Jesus compared God's gift of abundant life to water gushing up in a spring. Where fresh, cool water was scarce, what a marvelous comparison that was—a life that surged and bubbled with vitality, like life-sustaining water bubbling up from the rocks.

We settle too often for dry lives. We are afraid to give ourselves over to the surging joy of life that God offers. Yet Jesus continues to offer us the gift of new life, if we have the courage to accept it.

You lead us beside the waters, dear God. Help us accept your invitation to drink deeply. Amen.

I Am He

Read John 4:16–26.

The woman said to him, "I know that the Messiah is coming....Jesus said to her, "I am he, the one who is speaking to you" (John 4:25a, 26).

I never thought of my mother as disfigured. True, a pituitary tumor had made her hands, feet, and nose grow disproportionately large. This did make her shy and hesitant in new situations. Yet she was loving, generous, and caring. She loved to share with her friends her three-word sermon—"God is Love." When I was an adult attending her funeral, I was surprised to hear a relative speak of how brave she was, despite her disfigurement. Yet now I realize that in a culture that values physical beauty, she was something of an outcast. To me she was beautiful.

The disciples were shocked and embarrassed to see Jesus talking to an outcast. What an odd couple—a Jewish teacher and a sinful Samaritan woman! The two had verbally sparred for a while when Jesus called the woman to a true worship that would unify all. The woman affirmed that that would happen when the Messiah came. Then this Samaritan woman became the first person to hear Jesus actually say, "I am he"—the Messiah.

We all sometimes feel like outcasts. Yet God comes to us in our imperfection. Just as Paul celebrated that God could use Paul's weakness to show God's strength, we too can hear and share the good news. The Christ is with us.

Thank you, gracious God, for a reign of love in which all are equally precious before you. Amen.

The Fields Are Ripe

Read John 4:27–42.

"But I tell you, look around you, and see how the fields are ripe for harvesting" (John 4:35).

Knowles Shaw and his wife were musical evangelists for the Christian Church back in the 1880s. Joyous gospel music was a big part of their attractiveness, and they wrote new songs for that ministry. One was, "Bringing in the Sheaves."

Since grain isn't gathered by hand into sheaves anymore, we of today's generation aren't always clear what this song means. We smile at children singing, "bringing in the sheep," or even, "bringing in the sheets." And *sowing* does sound like *sewing*, doesn't it?

When we read John's Gospel, though, we hear the hymn for what it is—a joyful response to Christ's call for evangelism. The Samaritan woman seemed an unlikely candidate to become an evangelist. The disciples were shocked that Jesus would even talk with her, let alone treat her as an equal. Her reputation in the community must have been a real *reputation*. Yet she became not a bad example, but a model to the disciples of the urgent joy of spreading the gospel. She began where she was, spoke in honesty, and attracted others to Christ.

God can use us to invite others into faith. Our styles may differ from the woman at the well, or from Knowles Shaw, but this Lenten season may be a good time to consider our call. We've been given the living water, we've been given the secret of the Messiah. Shouldn't we share it?

Help us, dear God, share the love and acceptance that is so precious to us, that we may come rejoicing, bringing in the sheaves. Amen.

I Am Well Pleased!

Read Matthew 3:13–17.

"This is my Son, the Beloved, with whom I am well pleased" (Matthew 3:17).

My four-year-old grandson loves for me to tell him about the day he was born. We went to the hospital early in the morning because his Mommy was sure he was going to be born that day! When it was time for him to be born Momma (that's me) was in the delivery room with Mommy and saw Wayne the minute he was born. He was so beautiful! Papa and Aunt Heather and Uncle John and Aunt Trena were there to see him and we were all so happy! And God was happy that his special son Wayne was born.

Baptism and birth are alike. The waters of birth bring forth new life as we accept Jesus as our Savior and look forward to new life in that relationship. Each time we experience birth in the waters of baptism, we can hear the voice of God saying, "This is my beloved child." And I will look forward to the time when I can see my grandson's new birth in baptism.

As we see the symbols of baptism in our church, remind us that we are your children with whom you are pleased. Amen.

I Am the Bread of Life

Read John 6:22–40.

"I am the bread of life. Whoever comes to me will never be hungry…" (John 6:35).

According to John's Gospel, Jesus lived these words before he said them. A great crowd had followed, hungry for his teaching and healing. Soon physical hunger replaced spiritual hunger, and the disciples were frightened. How could they provide for the needs of this huge crowd? The teacher blessed a few fish and a few loaves that a boy in the crowd had offered, and a great multitude received their fill.

Then came questioning and comparing. Where did he come from? Who was he? What signs could he offer to prove his claims that he was sent by God? The questioners knew the story through their faith heritage of how Moses had provided manna in the wilderness. Could this feeding compare to that? Jesus then offered them some bread that was greater than manna—bread that would fill spiritual hunger and bring life to the world. Then he identified himself with the bread that God sent, saying, "I am the bread of life."

Each time we come to the communion table we live out the truth of this claim. Here, in the breaking of bread, we find a new source of life, nourishment, and strength. Reflect upon some moments when you have come to the Lord's table and have come away nourished. Those were moments when you affirmed Christ's claim to be the bread of life.

Thank you, God, for sending bread in our times of need. Amen.

Pass the Bread

Read John 6:25–32.

"It is my Father who gives you the true bread from heaven" (John 6:32).

Imagine stepping into a bakery about eight in the morning. The aroma of freshly baked bread is still in the air: a yeasty, sweet, warm smell. Bread is cooling in the various pans waiting to be sliced or wrapped. There are the pungent loaves of pumpernickel, round loaves of rye with caraway seeds, the flour-topped loaves of homestyle, and long loaves of sourdough, French, and Vienna.

Bread is a staple of our diet, a symbol of life. Wheat now combined, not threshed, milled, sold to the bakeries. Mixed with flour, eggs, milk, sugar, salt, shortening, and yeast as basic ingredients, it becomes a light loaf of bread. Bread is sustaining, nourishing, and filling.

Bread, unleavened—not given time to rise before fleeing Egypt. Manna on the grass, five barley loaves shared among a crowd with fragments left over. The bread of God, which comes down from heaven and gives us life. Jesus, the bread of life.

Thank you, God, for the metaphors in your Word that help us understand Jesus. For the physical enjoyment of eating bread and the reminder that Jesus is the sustainer of our lives, we offer our gratitude. Amen.

A Shipwreck Eucharist

Read Acts 27:9–44.

After he had said this, he took bread; and giving thanks to God in the presence of all, he broke it and began to eat (Acts 27:35).

If we read the verse above without reading the story around it, we might assume that it is a retelling of the Lord's Supper, or a picture of worship in the early church. Instead, it's the story of a meal aboard a sinking ship.

The story about the half-sunken ship wallowing in the waves reminds me of a movie I loved as a child—*The High and the Mighty*. Each time I watched it, I wished that stricken plane through the air on its course from Hawaii to San Francisco. To conserve fuel, they had to lighten the plane's load. Each of the passengers tossed their most precious belongings out the hatch.

Likewise, on Paul's stricken ship, listing low in the water, the crew had to throw overboard its load of wheat. Before that, however, Paul the prisoner had become the moral captain of the ship, giving orders and exhortations to keep the crew together in the crisis. At daybreak at the end of their second week afloat, Paul took bread, blessed it, broke it, and shared it with them. This simple act of sharing in a time of crisis must have reminded the person who wrote this story of the way Christ broke bread. The reader realizes that communion with the living Christ was taking place on that leaky boat, that the Christ who said "I am the bread of life" was going to keep them safe. When we break bread in difficult times, let us see in that act the promise of Christ's presence.

Be with us in breaking bread, living God, and encourage us when we are afraid of sinking in life's storms. Amen.

To Be Hungry. . .

Read John 6:25–35.
"He gave them bread from heaven to eat" (John 6:31).

In the mid-60s, I taught school in the inner city of Indianapolis. This school was in a transitional area where Appalachian folk moved after coming north to work in the factories. Needless to say, the families were poor. One day, Jenny didn't come to school. This was unusual, for she had a good attendance record.

The next day, she told me that none of her brothers or sisters had been in school because they had no food in the house. I asked, "Didn't someone have even enough money for a loaf of bread?" "No," she replied, "there was nothing."

That was my first realization that there is hunger in the world, in my city, in my school, right there in my schoolroom.

God gave manna to the Israelites in the wilderness; Jesus is the bread of life for all of us. What does that say to us—those of us who have so much more than just bread?

God, giver of manna and so much more, make us aware, and challenge us to see that others may have physical food as well as spiritual food. Amen.

An Interrupted Prayer

Read Luke 11:1–13.
"Give us each day our daily bread" (Luke 11:3).

A small group had gathered in the church parlor for a Saturday seminar on prayer. I was working through the Lord's Prayer with the group, when in wandered a transient. With a Santa Claus beard and ragged clothes, he was the perfect picture of an old-time hobo. He had hopped off a freight train and into our small community.

What could I do? Could I say, "Go away, leave us alone, I'm leading a seminar on prayer?" It was as if Jesus was looking over my shoulder, testing the teacher. The group took a break while I walked the man downtown to make arrangements for a meal. When I came back, the phrase "give us this day our daily bread" took on a new meaning for all of us at the seminar.

When we think of Jesus as the bread of life, we also remember his teachings about hospitality, about sharing bread. We may share out of obligation or embarrassment, as did the householder with his persistent midnight caller. We may share out of responsibility, as a parent shares good food with a child. But we remember that God shares out of pure love, inviting us to ask, to search, and to knock.

What can we hear from Jesus Christ about ways we can share the bread of life?

Help us find the faith to seek the bread you offer, O baker God; and help us find the love to share the bread that we receive. Amen.

Wednesday, March 10, 1993

Before Abraham Was, I Am

Read John 8:31–59.
Jesus said to them, "Very truly I tell you, before Abraham was, I am" (John 8:58).

Our Jewish brothers and sisters are a people tied to a story. Their story began with Abraham, who answered God's call into the unknown and became the father of three great faith traditions—Judaism, Christianity, and Islam. His spiritual descendents became numerous like the stars in the sky or the grains of sand on the seashore.

It's no wonder that Jewish leaders felt Jesus was presumptuous when he began making claims for himself. Even the great Abraham didn't offer eternal life. How could this ragtag carpenter?

John records a very strange response—one difficult to interpret. "Very truly I say to you, before Abraham was, I am." This claim not only seemed to elevate Jesus above Abraham, it tied him to Abraham's God—the one who told Moses, "I AM WHO I AM."

John did not record this episode to claim that Jesus was God, but to claim a oneness with God. John's Gospel began with a hymn to the Word, God's creative Spirit that moved over the waters at creation and that took on human flesh in Jesus Christ.

Such a claim confronts us on our Lenten journey. John described a Christ who lived before time and still lives today. What do we believe? How do we respond?

Let your Word that shaped the very world work within our hearts, O God, to help us discern who it is that we follow. Amen.

The Creator and the Christ

Read Genesis 1:1–3; John 1:1–3a.
In the beginning was the Word (John 1:1a).

The Hebrews had a word for spirit—it was *ruach*, a word that also referred to the wind, and to human breath. The Greeks had a word for spirit—it was *pneuma*, a word that also referred to the wind, and to human breath. The Spirit, in a way, was God's creative, life-giving urge; and along with it, the wisdom and power that brought order forth from chaos. Created in God's image, we possess something of that spirit—that life-force, that creativity.

The author of our Gospel identified the Spirit of Christ, which took human flesh in Jesus, as the same Spirit that was present when the light of the universe first was kindled. This Christ would promise his disciples a Spirit that would sustain them when he would no longer be with them (John 14:16). This Christ, risen from death, would breathe on them, bidding them to receive the Holy Spirit (John 20:22). God's creative, life-giving Spirit is still with us, renewing and refreshing us. Reflect upon ways that God's Spirit still blows in our midst.

Breathe on me, breath of God, fill me with life anew. Amen.

I Am the Light of the World

Read John 9:1–7.

"As long as I am in the world, I am the light of the world" (John 9:5).

We were deep underground, enjoying a cave tour. Spotlights played on the beautiful rock formations in a room large enough to be an underground cathedral. The guide smiled and asked us to put our hands a few inches in front of our faces. We complied. The guide threw a switch, plunging us into absolute darkness. We literally couldn't see the hands in front of our faces. The few seconds of darkness seemed like several minutes, and we all sighed in relief when the lights came back on and the tour resumed. We were grateful for light and the sense of sight by which we perceive it.

In such a trivial experience of relief and gratitude, we can well imagine what a stunning experience it must have been for the man born blind when the mud was washed from his eyes and light poured in. Thousands of images and colors filled his eyes. How had this happened? Whose touch had he felt? Whose was the voice that in the darkness said, "I am the light of the world..."?

Reflect upon the beauty and joy that light can bring. Don't take sight for granted, but celebrate it as a gift from God. Reflect upon the gracious act of Jesus in bringing sight to the one born blind, and pray that Christ's Spirit will enlighten your life in ever new and surprising ways.

Thank you for the gifts of light and sight, dear God. Thank you even more for the light that enters our lives in the love of Christ Jesus. Amen.

Saturday, March 13, 1993

A Light and a Sign

Read John 9:1–7, 24–41.

"If this man were not from God, he could do nothing" (John 9:33).

In 1923, an African American named Garrett Morgan invented the electric traffic light. It combined the ideas of a light, a sign, and a clock to help bring safety and order to traffic flow. We may mutter when stuck behind a red light, but we realize how frustrating, dangerous, and chaotic driving would be without it.

In bringing light and vision to a man born blind, Jesus lived out the claim that he was the light of the world. This act of healing became a sign—a signal that would help people see the love of God at work in this wandering teacher. More so than the other Gospels, John interprets the miracles of Jesus as signs demonstrating God's power and love. Where the disciples might have seen in the man's blindness a sign of sin, Jesus saw a sign of urgent opportunity—an opportunity for healing that would demonstrate that physical blindness is much less a problem than the spiritual blindness of those who choose not to see. The Gospel writer set the two forms of blindness in contrast to one another, and relished in the irony of setting in the role of teacher and witness the one who had previously been perceived as a victim and a sinner. At the same time, those who were supposed to be the teachers and leaders demonstrated the spiritual blindness that intolerance brings.

Let your light be a sign to us, O God, granting us insight and vision that we may follow your way. Amen.

The Light Shines in Darkness

Read John 1:1–4.

In him was life, and the life was the light of all people. The light shines in the darkness, and the darkness did not overcome it (John 1:4–5).

I picked up the phone in the dormitory hall to hear devastating news. The grandparents who had helped raise me were both killed in an auto accident. It was my first experience with the death of someone I loved; shock and grief enveloped me. My soul felt as if I were trapped in a dark whirlpool, pulling me toward death.

Was there hope to be found in the Bible? Those words from the beginning of John's Gospel had a strange, calming effect. God's love was working, reassuring me. The witness of Christ, the light that shines in darkness, is at least in part the assurance that God's love never lets go. That creative power of life, light, and hope is at work even in the darkest times. Through an almost-random encounter with scripture, I came to experience the light that indeed is the source and power of life.

The light shines in the darkness. God's steadfast love is at work even in the darkest moments that life can bring. God never abandons us or gives up on us, for God's love is stronger than death. In that we can find our own lives renewed, comforted, and strengthened.

Through Christ Jesus we can see the light of your love that shines in our deepest darkness. Thank you, God, for your steadfast love. Amen.

A Real Light

Read Revelation 21:21—22:6.

For the glory of God is its light, and its lamp is the Lamb (Rev. 21:23b).

Have you ever been outdoors on a clear night away from the city lights, pollution, and atmospheric conditions that obscure the heavens? Have you gazed at the Milky Way, the Big Dipper, seen Orion's Belt and the "W" made by Cassiopeia?

One evening several years ago we were coming back at night from a meeting; as we drove through the rural northwest Iowa countryside, the planet Venus was so bright that it looked as though it were an artificial light hung low in the sky.

Do you remember as a child seeing your first eclipse of the moon, or if you have been lucky, one of the sun? For a small period of time, a great heavenly body was hidden by another. How awe-inspiring a spectacle it is!

There is power in light, there is beauty in the light. God has created the heavens and their light for us as God has given Jesus for us—as our light.

> Fair is the sunshine,
> Fairer still the moonlight,
> And all the twinkling, starry host:
> Jesus shines brighter,
> Jesus shines purer,
> Than all the angels heaven can boast.

Creator of stars, moon, and sun, Creator of Jesus; thank you for the many lights in our life, especially the light of the world. Amen.

The Healing Light

Read John 1:1–18.

The light shines in the darkness and the darkness did not overcome it (John 1:5).

It seems as though light should be more of an Advent symbol than one for Lent. There are Advent candles, lights on Christmas trees, luminaries.

The Advent and Christmas scriptures from Isaiah and Luke are full of light images. And in the dark of winter, the image of light is welcome for our souls in many ways.

But it is Lent; Ash Wednesday has come, the days are getting longer, spring is around the corner. Why do we need light as a Lenten image? It seems incongruous for a symbol that is indicative of hope to be part of a season of penitence and suffering.

But if penitence is to sin what wholeness is to suffering, is there a more logical, meaningful symbol than light? How often do we forget that, even though Jesus has come, not all is light, but rather that there is now light in our darknesses? Perhaps that is the realistic hope in both Advent and Lent, a light in the darkness, "The light shines in the darkness and the darkness did not overcome it."

> In hope that sends a shining ray
> Far down the future's broadening way,
> In peace that only thou canst give,
> With thee, O Master, let me live.

God of darkness and God of light, we thank you for the hope you give in our darkness, for Jesus who sustains us in our darkness, and for the everlasting light. Amen.

You Can't Even Blow It Out!

Read Isaiah 60:1–3, 19–20.
The LORD will be your everlasting light (Isaiah 60:20).

One Sunday morning the pastor used a small birthday candle as an object for the children's sermon. After she had talked about Pentecost being the church's birthday, and celebrating with cake and candles, she asked one of the children to blow out the candle. The candle extinguished momentarily, and then to the children's amazement, it relit! They tried again and again to blow out the candle and it just wouldn't go out. The children's lesson was intended to help them understand that the Holy Spirit is always with us, as the flame of the candle was lit and would not go out.

Isaiah used the metaphor of light to give hope to the Israelites. "Arise, shine; for your light has come," he told them, contrasting the darkness with the light. "Your sun shall no more go down,...the LORD will be your everlasting light" (Isaiah 60:1, 20).

The birthday candle will not be blown out; even its tiny flame will put light into darkness. There is everlasting hope with God's light, God's Son, the Light of the world. We are assured that this light will never go out.

God, giver of light and hope, shine in our darkness. Let this light remind us always of your presence in our lives. Amen.

Is It Always Light up Here?

Read Colossians 1:9–14.

...joyfully giving thanks to the Father, who has enabled you to share in the inheritance of the saints in the light (Colossians 1:11b–12).

Perhaps it was something I was supposed to have learned in fifth grade science class, but I hadn't. It was a cloudy dark day as the plane left Lambert Field in St. Louis; I almost felt claustrophobic as the plane ascended into that dark mass with no scenery below. There was nothing but moist clouds—no break, no light.

But as we climbed to our "cruising altitude," as the pilots always say, I was in for a surprise. There, above the dark clouds, was the sun, clear blue sky, and *light*. I didn't know it was that way. I had somehow missed the science lesson that would have explained it to me.

The clear sky above the clouds has remained an important metaphor for me since that experience. In spite of disappointments, suffering, despair, and darkness, above it all is light and God's love. Above the dark clouds, there is clear sky and light. God has rescued us from the powers of darkness.

This doesn't mean life will be easy, but life can be bearable. Fred Craddock sums it up, "...not because Christ came, there will be no more suffering, but because there is suffering, there is Christ." The light will always be there above the clouds.

At times, O God, our lives seem filled with darkness, despair, and suffering. Help us to remember that Jesus is the light of the world; we have been rescued from the darkness. Amen.

I Am the Gate for the Sheep

Read John 10:1–10.

So again Jesus said to them, "Very truly I tell you, I am the gate for the sheep" (John 10:7).

It is late in the evening, and I am alone in an office building. The security system has been turned on. If anyone enters, alarms will ring here and at the security agency. To leave, I will have to turn off the alarm system momentarily and re-arm it so the building will remain safe. Because of the alarm system and the locked doors, I don't worry that the rest of the building is dark and empty.

There were many people who opposed Jesus and who would later threaten the young Christian community. There were many ideas that could seduce and turn people away from their faith in Jesus as the Christ. So the Gospel writer used this teaching of Jesus to both warn and encourage the young church. Entrenched political and religious forces would attack the Christian community as a threat to the established powers. Teachers with different ideas would try to come in the back door, acting like wolves in sheep's clothing. To counteract such threats, we have the image of Jesus standing at the gate, even functioning as the gate, to guard and protect the sheep. Where others would seek to destroy, Jesus seeks to bring life beyond measure.

We each have our security systems that bring us a sense of safety in a dangerous world. We each have ultimate security as we accept the life that Christ offers.

Guard us when we are endangered, encourage us when we are frightened, be our security when we ourselves are weak. Help us learn to trust that you are the good shepherd. Amen.

A Doorkeeper

Read Psalm 84.

I would rather be a doorkeeper in the house of my God than live in the tents of wickedness (Psalm 84:10b).

Sometimes when I open the door at church or at work for people who are coming with their hands full, that verse will pop into my mind. Sometimes I'll quote it with a smile. Other times I'll groan to myself that a "doorkeeper's" salary isn't enough to cover basic bills, while the wicked do quite well for themselves—but even then I'll realize that being in God's business brings rewards that can't be measured.

Days when we joyously celebrate the goodness of God add more meaning to our lives than do years of humdrum activity. The richness of God's presence is more rewarding than the financial gain we might have by giving our lives over to compromise with those who "live in the tents of wickedness." In terms of both time and wealth the psalmist reminds us that quality is more important than quantity. Trusting in God and centering our lives on God's love, then, brings abundant life and true joy. The Christ who called himself the "door" watches over those of us who are called to be doorkeepers.

A day in your presence is better than a thousand elsewhere, dear God. Help us learn to enjoy your presence. Amen.

I Am the Good Shepherd

Read John 10:11–15.

"I am the good shepherd. The good shepherd lays down his life for the sheep" (John 10:11).

The tornado went up the main street of town, uprooting trees, twisting roofs, exploding windows, shattering walls. In just a few moments, homes, businesses, and church buildings had been tossed around like toys in a nursery.

Electric lines were down. Furnaces couldn't run, because the electric blowers were powerless. People huddled together in the cold night that followed the storm, sharing food by candlelight. Telephone service was nonexistent.

The next morning, the young pastor was perplexed. How were the members of his congregation? Who was injured? Who was homeless? How were people reacting to stress and trauma? What could be salvaged from the crumbling church building? There was only one way to find out. He walked miles around the town, for the streets were blocked with downed trees. He stepped over electric lines that lay across the sidewalks. He listened to people's stories, as they tried to make sense out of the terrible storm that disrupted their lives.

This pastor wasn't particularly brave and heroic. He needed the reassurance and support of the church members, as much as they needed his. He was a pastor, though—the word means *shepherd*. A frightened flock needed him. What else could he do, and still be true to the one who is the good shepherd of all Christians?

Savior, like a shepherd lead us, for much we need thy tender care. Amen.

Never Alone

Read Matthew 18:10–14.

"I am the good shepherd. I know my own and my own know me" (John 10:14).

I just love Annie Vallotton's line illustrations in the Good News Bible. She has captured with a few simple lines the very essence of scripture passages.

My favorite is the illustration from Matthew 18 where Jesus is telling about a shepherd counting only ninety-nine sheep from his flock of a hundred. The responsible shepherd goes and looks for the stray and rejoices as it is found. The illustration from this teaching is like a children's picture-find puzzle. You know the kind. There is an intricate drawing and a list of "hidden" pictures to find.

Ms. Vallotton has a shepherd peering into dense bushes looking for the sheep. The leaves on the bushes are rippled and curly. Deep in these bushes is the lamb, asleep and curled within the bushes, his wool rippled and curly like the bush.

The message of such a shepherd who always will find his sheep and will know his sheep is of such comfort to those who have been abused or abandoned as children. These scriptures speak of a loving shepherd, a parent who will not abandon, but will always seek out and find the child. This message of "being sought" can be a new awakening to those who have been cast aside.

Thank you, God, for new messages of love and acceptance that have the power to change peoples lives. We know that Jesus will always be present in our lives; for that reassurance we are grateful! Amen.

Lead Us Good Shepherd

Read Psalm 23.

He leads me in right paths for his name's sake (Psalm 23:3b).

Have you ever seen, either live or on television, a border collie work the sheep? The dogs are a Scottish breed and have highly developed instincts for shepherding. Coupled with training, they are very reliable caretakers for sheep. Although the sheep may want to scatter in all directions, the dogs, crouching close to the ground and turning quickly, are able to keep the sheep together and going in the right direction.

In the hymn, "Father Almighty, Bless Us with Thy Blessing," the words echo the shepherd of the Psalms:

Shepherd of souls, who bringest all who seek thee
To pastures green beside the peaceful waters,
Tenderest guide, in ways of cheerful duty
Lead us, good Shepherd.

God the good Shepherd leads us beside the right paths. Jesus the good Shepherd knows his sheep. So often we do not follow God's ways. But as a border collie always keeps the sheep from straying, our belief in Jesus keeps us on the right path.

God, it is reassuring to know that, as difficult as life is, we have you to always keep us from straying. Thank you for your shepherding ways. Amen.

Feed My Sheep

Read John 21:15–19.
Jesus said to him, "Tend my sheep" (John 21:16b).

We thank thee that thy church, unsleeping
While earth rolls onward into light,
Through all the world her watch is keeping,
And rests not now by day or night.

Jesus' instructions to Peter and the disciples were to tend and feed his sheep. Jesus, as our shepherd, nourished us and now in turn, as heirs of Peter and the church, it is up to us to feed and tend the sheep.

Over all the world, manifestations of tending and feeding take place night and day without rest, without pause. Food relief is lifted into war-torn countries. In base communities in South and Central America, the church offers sanctuary for the persecuted, continuing its message in spite of danger. In areas damaged by natural disasters, food, money, health supplies, and clothing are sent. Shelters are set up in churches, city and suburban, for the homeless. The word of God is proclaimed in the prisons. Volunteers help make the last days of those dying from AIDS less isolated.

The world goes on, but the church unsleeping keeps on tending and feeding the sheep. Where, what, and how are you challenged to be a part of this?

Help us each to find a way, O God, to help your church proclaim your love to all the world. Amen.

I Am the Resurrection and the Life

Read John 11:17–44.

"I am the resurrection and the life. Those who believe in me, even though they die, will live" (John 11:25).

Most of us can recall hearing these words spoken at funerals and graveside services. They helped us offer up to God a life we held precious. The words are appropriate and fitting, and point us to our hope in Christ.

When the words were first spoken, however, they were a shock and a surprise. Jesus had told Martha that her dead brother Lazarus would rise again. Martha affirmed her faith in a resurrection that would be a future event. Jesus, however, claimed that the resurrection wasn't a future event, but a present person. In him was the power of new life. After making this claim, he challenged Martha—"Do you believe this?" Martha responded with a great confession of faith. Again, Jesus not only made a claim, but acted it out in calling Lazarus forth from the tomb.

In this story, Martha had many conflicting and perplexing feelings and was trying to deal with them in the light of her faith in God and Christ. Jesus guided her, as the living Christ can guide us, in a process of sorting through feelings, doubts, and beliefs, to a point where we too can confess, "Yes, Lord, I believe that you are the Messiah."

When life seems difficult and full of death, help guide us into a deeper faith, dear God. Amen.

Cassie's Baptism

Read Romans 6:5–11.

For if we have been united with him in a death like his, we will certainly be united with him in a resurrection like his (Romans 6:5).

The young pastor hadn't known Cassie long at the time of her funeral, but he knew her well. Though over ninety, she had been a delightful person to visit. At her funeral, he couldn't help but recall a story she told.

Young Cassie had decided one spring to accept Jesus as her savior. Like Martha in the Bible, she confessed that faith. She looked forward with eagerness to the day of her baptism when the church would gather at a farm pond. There were two problems. It was a cold spring, and ice was still present on the northern Iowa pond. And Cassie had not been a healthy child—she often had respiratory ailments. Shouldn't she wait for warmer weather? No, even if it killed her, she was going to be baptized. They broke the ice from the pond and she went down into the cold water. Eighty years later, she told the pastor with a smile and a wink that she was always healthy as a horse after that.

For most of us, baptism is symbolic of death and new life in Christ. For Cassie it had been a commitment that was more than symbolic. She truly believed in the one who said, "I am the resurrection and the life."

Help us reclaim our baptism, O God of new life, and renew our commitment to the living Christ. Amen.

I Am the Way, and the Truth, and the Life

Read John 14:1–14.

Thomas said to him, "…How can we know the way?" Jesus said to him, "I am the way, and the truth, and the life" (John 14:5b–6a).

My scenic routes are legendary in the family. My shortcuts usually only take us ten miles out of the way. It hurts my male ego to stop and ask for directions—I'm always sure that if we go just a little farther, we'll find that cross street. Well, maybe.

Like me, Thomas the disciple usually assumed he knew where he was going. He was passionately loyal to Jesus, but still stubbornly dependent on his own understanding. Finally, after hearing some vague and confusing words about Jesus going to his father's house, Thomas gave up. He blurted out his need for clearer directions. Jesus responded that *he* was the way, the truth, and the life. Through Jesus, Thomas could find the way to a loving God. Thomas's people had been given a way. The *Torah*, a word we translate as *law*, literally means *the way*. Through it, Jews could learn the truth, and find the life that God offered. Now Jesus was taking upon himself the role that the law had played.

What kind of way does Jesus Christ offer us? How can the Christ help us learn the truth about God and receive the gift of life? Let these questions guide us on our journey.

Be our way, our truth, and our life, O God in Christ, and let us follow you faithfully. Amen.

Love Letters

Read John 14:1–4, 15–24.

"And if I go and prepare a place for you, I will come again and will take you to myself, so that where I am, there you may be also" (John 14:3).

It was a difficult parting, but necessary. We were engaged. One of us had to stay and finish college. The other had to go three hundred miles away to begin seminary. Only after a year of separation would marriage be feasible. It was discouraging for both of us, but daily letters kept us going. We shared the little things, the big problems, and mostly, our feelings for one another. Those love letters helped us survive until we could be together again.

A scholar who wrote the study notes in my New Oxford Annotated Bible said of the 14th through the 17th chapters of John, "It is a meditation, which—like a love letter—is difficult to outline." It is also like a love letter in that Jesus is teaching the disciples what his love is all about. These discourses were designed to give the disciples strength and hope during troubled times. If they loved their Christ, they would stay true to him and love one another. This love would prepare them for the ultimate reunion, in the eternal love of God. Even when their beloved teacher would be hauled away to the cross, this love should keep them together. How do we answer God's love letters?

Dear God, we can hardly comprehend your love for us; help us learn to love you and one another more each day. Amen.

Words of Advice

Read Philippians 4:4–9.

What does the LORD require of you but to do justice, and to love kindness, and walk humbly with your God?(Micah 6:8).

I would be true, for there are those who trust me;
I would be pure, for there are those who care;
I would be strong, for there is much to suffer;
I would be brave, for there is much to dare.

Like a blueprint, words of advice, or a road map, the scripture and the hymn give active, growing Christians suggestions for living out the Christian life. How can we help hunger and homelessness? What can we do to help carry out love and justice? Where do we need to be brave and truthful to carry out Jesus' commandment to love one another? Where do we need to rejoice more, pray more?

The Christian way, with Jesus as our guide, is a process. We never arrive, but are constantly on the path of action.

Paul tells us to keep on doing the things we have learned, and we will be rewarded by the assurance that the God of peace will be with us.

Lead us in service and prayer and rejoicing as we journey on the Christian way. Thank you, God, for your guidance. Amen.

Life's Instructions

Read Exodus 20:1–17.

Your word is a lamp to my feet and a light to my path (Psalm 119:105).

One of the books on the best seller list these days is called, *Life's Little Instruction Book*. The author, H. Jackson Brown, Jr., wrote the book for his son. Like all parents, Mr. Brown decided he needed to give his son some advice as he left home for college. The result is a book of many kinds of sage advice. He says in the introduction that "It...was...the responsibility of the parents to provide a road map for their children."

That is what God gave Moses, as he was about to lead God's children through the wilderness—a road map. Here was a list of rules, commandments for a relationship between God and God's people. Throughout generations, the Israelites followed this law. It is reiterated and celebrated in Psalm 119. Jesus gave a new direction to God's laws as he reinterpreted them in the New Testament. Ultimately Jesus is the way as the word and law of God.

Throughout generations, Christians have followed these same laws; our instruction book is God's law; actually written by our father for us: God's children.

O Word of God incarnate, O Wisdom from on high,
O Truth unchanged, unchanging, O Light of our
    dark sky;
We praise thee for the radiance that from the
    hallowed page,
A lantern to our footsteps, shines on from age to
    age.

For not setting us in the world without guidance and a way to live, we thank you, God. Amen.

I Am the Vine, You Are the Branches

Read John 15:1–17.

"As the Father has loved me, so I have loved you; abide in my love" (John 15:9).

It was Sunday morning, and I was boarding an airliner to fly to a strange city for a business meeting. I was lonely already and frustrated at not being able to be with my faith family at worship. The only litany I heard was the flight attendant's cheerful recital of what to do in case of a disaster.

My mood darkened as I leaned against the window. The plane hurtled into the sky. Below, my eyes caught the familiar patterns of suburban streets. Wait...there's my church's neighborhood! My eye caught the upswept roofline of the sanctuary, and I felt a part of the worship even though I was apart from it. I reflected upon God's gift of connectedness, and thanked God as the plane went on its way.

Jesus used a familiar analogy to illustrate the way that God, the Christ, and Christians are all connected. Vine and branches, abiding in one another, loving as we have been loved, all became part of the farewell discourse. We are one with God and with one another. Reflect upon some of the wide variety of Christians around the world with whom you are connected through the vine of God's love. Rejoice that we are never truly apart from that love.

When we would lose track of our connectedness, dear God, help us realize that you are the vine, and we are the branches. Amen.

Thursday, April 1, 1993

The Seeds Sprouted!

Read Isaiah 55:10–13.

"For as the rain and the snow come down from heaven,…making it bring forth and sprout…" (Isaiah 55:10).

One fall day, four-year-old Heather and her little friend Tanya took some fat green beans that had been left on the vines and picked them. They decided to play gardener, taking the seeds from inside the pod and planting them at the edge of the garden.

During the long winter, they forgot about this. They, along with their mothers, were surprised the next spring to see beans coming up at the edge of the garden where none had been planted yet. The rain, the snow, and the cold Iowa winter hadn't deterred the beans from growing.

Jesus is the vine, we are the branches. We are assured that the rain will come to us in many forms to water us, making us bring forth and sprout. We too can be surprised, as were the girls, by what is growing.

God who sends rain, let it fall on us to make us bring forth and sprout with your love. Amen.

Our Identity, Our Responsibility

Read 1 Peter 2:2–11.

"Once you were not a people, but now you are God's people" (1 Peter 2:10).

What wonderful words this epistle gives Christians! How important we're made to feel. But these words are not lightly given. They follow a list of instructions for living the Christian life: get rid of malice, guile, insincerity, envy, and slander. Having done this, our growth in salvation can continue.

That, however, is not the end of our Christian development. We have been chosen by God to be God's people. We are connected. Jesus said, "I am the vine, you are the branches." We are connected so that we can proclaim the mighty acts of who called us out of darkness.

Well, then, where do we begin? Christianity isn't an armchair sport. It is a belief of hands, heart, voice, and feet. We need to be witnessing, sharing our faith story. We can be knitting, building, baking, serving. We can be visiting, comforting, listening, and caring. We can be taking, moving, and clearing.

What wonderful news to be someone—God's someone. God's people. We must remember that this wonderful news cannot be kept to one's self.

We confess that as your people, we are guilty of keeping this wonderful news to ourselves all too often. Remind us that we must act on this news as we claim our identity in Jesus the vine. Amen.

Saints in Squeaky Pews

Read 1 Thessalonians 5:12.

Respect those who labor among you,...esteem them very highly in love because of their work (1 Thessalonians 5:12, 13).

Each time I sing the last verse of a communion hymn, deep in my memory I hear the back pew squeak. It has been many years since I was a youth in my home church but the memory is still real. The elders and deacons would sit in the back pew during worship. While the communion hymn was being sung, they stood in unison to walk to the front of the sanctuary. As they stood, the pew invariably squeaked.

These were the leaders in my home church. They were elders, deacons, church school teachers, youth fellowship sponsors, committee chairpersons. They were respected in the church community as they did God's work. I still see faces, remember names, and esteem them highly, recalling Paul's words. They were influential in my faith development.

We are called as God's people; we are called as branches of the vine. Remember those who were influential in your faith development. Give thanks for their love in Jesus Christ. Search your own life. Probably more than you know, you are helping someone else's faith story grow.

We praise you God for those in our lives who have helped us grow in faith. Let us pass that faith on to others. Amen.

From Comfort to Challenge

Read John 12:9–19.

"Hosanna! Blessed is the one who comes in the name of the Lord" (John 12:13).

Do you have early memories of vacation church school? Does the very smell of grape Kool-Aid and butter cookies with the hole in the middle bring back impressions of early summer mornings as you sat around the little tables in small chairs? Can you remember the comfortable feeling of being a part of the "Bible school"—as it was called then?

"Tell Me the Stories of Jesus" was one of the songs many of us learned as youngsters in church. The words made us feel as though we were right there at Jesus' knee—just as the song says. It was such a comforting song, as well it should be. But here is the third verse.

> Into the city I'd follow
> The children's band,
> Waving a branch of a palmtree
> High in my hand;
> One of His heralds,
> Yes, I would sing
> Loudest hosannas,
> "Jesus is King!"

Read the words carefully. What comes next in the story? The comfort and presence of Jesus has turned into a parade with a dramatic ending. Where will you be at the middle of the week—still at Jesus' knee in the garden? We are challenged!

God, give us strength as we are challenged daily to live for you. We know that comfort and ease are not always present; help us we pray. Amen.

Our Power

Read 2 Timothy 1:6–10.

For God did not give us a spirit of cowardice, but rather a spirit of power and of love and of self-discipline (2 Timothy 1:7).

Sunday August 30, 1992. I am reading the Sunday Post-Dispatch. St. Louis High in Murders. Priest Accused of Sexual Abuse. Boy, twelve, missing in storm sewer filled by heavy rain. Millions of kids go hungry during the summer because of the summer break from school lunch programs. Prosecutor misused office funds. One hundred eighty thousand left homeless in Florida from Hurricane Andrew. Enough? I haven't begun to touch the international news!

Our church school today was listing the problems in the world in one column on the chalkboard and the solutions offered by the church in another. Power was listed as one of the solutions. In the letter to Timothy, we are reminded that God didn't give us a lack of courage, but rather power and love. Our church school class couldn't solve the world's problems, nor could yours. But we can be aware of our power, our source of power in God. We are called with a holy calling, the letter continues, according to God's purpose and grace; we may need to suffer for the gospel, relying on the power of God.

As we get discouraged reading the paper, hearing and seeing the news of our day, we need to remember the words of Jesus, "I am the way," and our power as followers of the way. What can we be empowered to do in our world with this source?

There is so much for Christians to do in the world today to show your love and care for all people. Show us our power in action. Amen.

Tuesday, April 6, 1993

From a Dead Vine, New Possibilities

Read Isaiah 11:1–9.

A shoot shall come out from the stump of Jesse, and a branch shall grow out of his roots (Isaiah 11:1).

It was early spring in our first parsonage and I was eager to get the yard in shape. I began by cutting dead branches from overgrown bushes and vines in the flower bed. There seemed to be a lot of vines that were for all intents and purposes dead. I finally asked someone if they knew what these were. "Clematis," I was told. "They have lovely purple flowers and grow up trellises." I quit cutting those dead vine and waited for their lovely purple flowers.

From the seemingly dead vines came green shoots, leaves, and star-shaped flowers. From a stump of Jesse comes a shoot and a branch from the roots. From the dead comes life.

All sorts of dead, impossible things can happen. A ruler can judge not by what is seen or heard, but with righteousness. The enemy of the meek shall lie down with them as the image Isaiah so vividly gives us. And the vulnerable child will be near the snake and not hurt.

'I am the vine, you are the branches," Jesus tells us. Are our vines dead and need to be pruned out, or are they only dormant like the clematis vine and need revitalizing? What in our lives can live again? What possibilities do our new growing lives offer to others?

"Help us to grow, O God. Let us grow in our faith to you and our responsibility to others. We are thankful that with you impossible things can happen. Amen.

The Home Place

Read John 14:1–7.

"In my Father's house there are many dwelling places" (John 14:2a).

On a hot August day, we buried my uncle. He had lived all of his married life on a farm near a small Midwest town. The funeral was held in a town north of where he had farmed.

As we drove with the funeral procession to the cemetery where his wife, parents, and several sisters were buried, the route took us past the very place he had farmed for so many years. I was deeply moved by the significance. For the last time, my uncle was going by the place which had been home on route to the place where he would be interred.

The words from John's Gospel came to me, "In my Father's house are many dwelling places." My uncle had lived in one dwelling place for most of his life. Now he journeyed to another dwelling place with God. Jesus told his disciples that the route to this dwelling place was through him: "I am the way."

God, giver of homes, both here on earth and with you eternally, help us follow your way as our belief in Jesus is strengthened. Amen.

This Is My Body

Read 1 Corinthians 11:23–26.
"This is my body that is for you"(1 Corinthians 11:24).

Lord, at thy table we behold
The wonders of thy grace;
But, most of all, admire that we
Should find a welcome place.

Try this: read the scripture from 1 Corinthians and put your own name in the sentence. It will go like this: This is my body that is for you, David (or Betty, or Andy). Think of the significance of personal worth, of the individualization which that statement takes on.

God's grace is for all, saint and sinner, bound and free, confident and reticent, loved and forsaken. God's son is for all; he died for us, his body was broken for all of us. That love symbolized by the broken bread is for each of us individually.

What a wonderful assuring message of love and acceptance and freedom that is for those who are or have been prisoners of abandonment or abuse. There are those among us, or even we ourselves, who find it hard to believe that they are lovable and capable because they have heard so many messages to the contrary. Yet, in this context, "This is my body that is for you," how much easier it is to recognize self-worth.

For new messages in our lives that give us a sense of loveability and worth, we thank you God. We accept your gift of grace. Amen.

The Leavings

Read Psalm 34:1–10.
> *O taste and see that the LORD is good* (Psalm 34:8).

Martin Luther King, Sr. had a favorite expression in the word *leavings*. He had learned this word from his mother and preached on it many times. Even after the senior King had lost two sons and a wife, who was slain while playing the organ one Sunday, he believed that life always has enough left to make it worth living.

This psalm is about God's *providence*, a rather difficult theological term on which to get a handle.

Perhaps one way to grasp it is to say that, ultimately, God is in charge! The writer of the psalm gives credence to how God is in charge of his life.

Being secure in God's providence, it is easier to remember the "leavings"—that which is left over to make it all worthwhile. The crucifixion was an event that seemed to have no leavings, nothing left to make life worth living. But in the providence of God, bad news is never the final news. Jesus said, "I am the resurrection and the life." The providence of God is indeed evident and we can take up the leavings and go on, witnessing that the Lord is good!

Thank you for being in charge, O Lord. Let us be aware of the many leavings for which we have to be thankful. Amen.

Those Who Wait

Read Isaiah 40:28–31.

Those who wait for the LORD shall renew their strength (Isaiah 40:31).

It is Saturday. Good Friday was not good after all. The leader was dead—killed, executed in a most horrible fashion. The band of followers was scattered, in shock and disbelief that something like this could happen to God's son.

What now? The new way of life, the teaching, the healing, the miracles, relationships—all had soured in the light of the new developments. O God, it wasn't supposed to happen like this.

In a whirlwind of fast-moving events, betrayal, arrest, trial, beatings, crowds, shouting, confusion, and finally the crucifixion, somehow the scenario seemed without a script. What could happen now?

Isaiah says the Lord is an everlasting God. A biblical scholar puts the despair of that Saturday into words for Easter Sunday: "The resurrection can only be received and affirmed and celebrated as the new action of God whose province it is to create new futures for people and let them be *amazed* in the midst of despair."* We know the ending (or is it the beginning?) of the story. Sunday follows Saturday, and once more things are put into perspective.

In the midst of our hopelessness, let us be amazed as we wait for the Lord. Amen.

---

* Brueggeman, Walter, *The Prophetic Imagination*. Philadelphia: Fortress, 1978, p. 107.

The Sonrise

Read Matthew 28:1–10.

After the Sabbath, as the first day of the week was dawning, Mary Magdalene and the other Mary went to see the tomb (Matthew 28:1).

What is your favorite picture on an Easter worship bulletin? Is it lilies, trumpets suggesting the heralding of the Easter message, or a scene at the empty tomb? As I look at the choices each year for Easter bulletins, I am drawn to the ones with the sunrise.

After a Good Friday in darkness and a Saturday of doubt, uncertainty, and fear, Sunday dawns. None of the Gospels tell us that the sun was brilliant in the sky; Matthew comes the closest by saying that the day was dawning. But even without a vivid description of a sunrise of many colors, we get the picture. The tomb is empty. There Jesus isn't!

At the raising of Lazarus, Jesus said, "I am the resurrection." Now, at his own tomb, he is the resurrected. The day dawns, anew, afresh, and with new meaning. Life has conquered death. The sun rises gloriously over an empty tomb!

> As the sun doth daily rise
> Brightening all the morning skies,
> So to thee with one accord
> Lift we up our hearts, O Lord!

For daybreak and sunrise, constant reminders of life eternal, we do lift up our hearts, O Lord, in praise and thanksgiving. Amen.

Hymns Quoted

Guide Me, O Thou Great Jehovah
                    William Williams, 1745

Fairest Lord Jesus
                    Münster Gesangbuch, 1677;
                    trans. Joseph A. Seiss, 1873

O Master, Let Me Walk with Thee
                    Washington Gladden, 1879

Father Almighty, Bless Us with Thy Blessing
                    Berwick Hymnal, 1886

The Day Thou Gavest, Lord, Is Ended
                    John Ellerton, 1870

I Would Be True
          Howard Arnold Walter, (1883-1918)

O Word of God Incarnate
                    William How, 1867

Tell Me the Stories of Jesus
                    William H. Parker, 1885

Lord, at Thy Table We Behold
                    Joseph Stennett, (1663-1713)

As the Sun Doth Daily Rise
     Latin hymn, adapt. Horatio Nelson, 1864